The Ink In My Scars

Jade Melissa Stuart

1

Gently turn my pages,
As each page peels back
A layer
Of my experiences
And
My protection.

Handle With Care

ISBN-13:
978-1548830038

ISBN-10:
1548830038

Content:

The Scars

She was the type they called quiet,
She was undecided on their intentions.
So remained like an unopened flower
Withholding all her beauty
From the world.
Indecisive about opening up
To the wrong conditions.
Afraid it could ruin everything
She worked so hard on inside.
Whilst equally afraid that
She may be the only one to ever see it.

It felt like everything
And nothing all at the same time.
It pulled every emotion
Through my pours so painfully
Making me relive every second on repeat.
Whilst leaving me feeling numb
And dead behind my eyes.
I could almost hear the little girl
Inside me crying to break free from
The internal prison that we never saw coming
But here we was in this hell together.
The little girl inside me
Never did leave, I often remembered
Her happiness in moments like this.
Whilst I pleaded to feel anything but
Everything and nothing all at once.
I begged to feel happy once again.

Call me a feminist if you must,
If it helps you sleep at night.
If it helps your sorry existence feel more entitled
To everything you already have.
It must be difficult to eat from a silver spoon
When you believe you deserve gold.
Whilst everyone else eats from the ground.
It's burdensome to you that I point this out
When you need the clean smooth road of privilege to be
free from peasants.
No amount of trauma could change your stance, if it is
separate from you.
I'm sorry if my black skin and female anatomy offend
your blissful life,
And make you listen to things that do not concern your
way of life.
How nice it would be to be burden-less upon society.
How wonderful is ignorance when
Ignorance is bliss.

Excuses, excuses, excuses,
They always caused me
The most pain.
I could handle the truth,
But you didn't think I was deserving.
Excuses are what I was
Always given
For your damaging behaviour.
Kindly holding my hand
Leading me into the darkness
And leaving me there.
To find my own way out.
All because your ego is
More important than your morals.

Not everyone is tuned in
To understand you.
You are not made
To be everybody's.
That does not make you
Any less valuable,
That just makes you,
Unfound.
You cannot teach him
To understand you.
He has to want too.
You do not need to beg
Or show him ways
To love you.
The truth is overbearing
In both of your eyes.
You have both
Settled for less than
Your heart desires.

I always thought
That letting someone
Inside you
Was a different level of intimacy.
Turns out it wasn't intimate at all.
It was a brief rest on their journey
Out of your life.
It was a way to use you
For their needs.
Then degrade you for giving in.
A way to make you feel filthy
Right down to your core.

Although you made it very clear
Who you expected her to be.
You offered her no reason
To grant your wish.
You demanded paradise
Whilst you offered bedlam.
You forgot that flowers
Do not grow in concrete jungles.

I gazed on watching the sound from my lips funnel
Into your ears like many times before.
This time I expected to be ignored,
Everyone knew you only did things for the benefit of
yourself.
Whilst we continued to feed the beast of your ego,
I began to starve.
I had to leave you alone to fend for yourself
Knowing one of two things would happen.
You would learn a hard lesson of life or
You would find someone else to stroke your ego.
I knew what I wanted but I also knew the truth.

As I write under my sheets and under my skin,
I feel less exposed whilst I peel back my layers,
Less vulnerable to the judgment of the world.
My safe place,
The same place that protected me from the monsters of
my childhood.
In that not much has changed.
Except for the person who is
No longer a child but is still afraid of the world outside
her sheets.

Sometimes you must decide
Between finding yourself
Or finding yourself in him.
I know which one makes you smile
But remember
Which one is guaranteed?

I either felt too deeply
Or not at all
I either felt too passionately
Or I felt numb.
I didn't get to decide,
It choose me.
It would creep up and
Decide to play host.
Possessing my body like a puppet
With its master.

A lightning bolt through my chest,
That stress, that worry, that anxiety.
It has almost become a friend
It was so frequently around.
It was almost a reminder that I'm alive
Away from the numb dark room of my mind,
The seesaw of swinging from one to the other.
Neither was kind to me but I desperately longed to feel
something.
Although I felt glued down I never lost hope
That my pain
Would give me the strength to grow wings.

I watched you as the pain took over
And your eyes began to fill
With the overflow.
You knew you had to let go
But you questioned every moment after.
You often wondered
If it was the right thing to do.
The truth is you cannot let go
Of something that is holding on to you.
It was never you who needed to fight a little harder.
You was always enough,
He just was not man enough to carry you.
He let go long before you did.

If you're not reading carefully
Sometimes you read a word differently
And it changes the whole meaning
Of the text you just read.
People are like that.
If you're not listening carefully,
If you listen selectively
And interpret how you wish,
You might not know them at all.

If when you fell in love,
You needed to be less like you.
You're the only one who fell,
That's not love.
That's the devil in cupids clothing.

Sometimes I liked to leave parts of myself
Out of my conversations,
So people couldn't track my thoughts
Or understand all of me.
A way of protecting myself.
A way of staying in control.
Then if I was rejected
I told myself that they never really knew me.
That helped me,
I think.

I see you.

You, the person that hides those parts of yourself that you think can't be loved.

The secrets, the facades, the masks.

I see you whole,

As the perfectly imperfect person you are.

You have been taught that as long as you be the person they need you to be

You will be loved.

Your fire still burns and the light in your eyes are still glowing.

Do not let anyone dim your glow and put out your fire.

We are all broken
In one way or another,
We all break the same.
From the moment
We are born we experience
Someone else's truth
Conflicting with our own.
Everyone tells you
Their truth is the only truth
And you accept that.
Until your heart pleads
With you to stop
Hurting yourself over and over.
Till you stop and listen.
Till the faintest of whisper
Becomes loud and clear.
Till you see you.

Isn't it disappointing that we are given
A mind of our own
A voice of our own
To then hand the power over to the intangible.
Whether it be fate, karma or something else
That someone told you about one time.
Who said you didn't have the power to decide
What was right for you?
Who decided you couldn't use your voice
To fight for you?
Who convinced you that something else
Decided your time on earth?
Who said that?

She always held a place in her heart,
Hopeful that the good
In him would pull through.
That person he presented to her
At his own convenience,
For his own convenience.
She listened to him apologise again
For repeatedly doing the same thing.
For repeatedly choosing himself
Over someone who also chose him.
There was no way he would let
A situation that good just go.
And her heart was too forgiving
To accept that some people
Just aren't what you want them to be.

At first it wasn't visible
But now I watched it
Practically drip from your lips.
You could hide it
But you couldn't escape its
Hold on you.
It changed the way you looked
And it changed you.
You lost the control
That you so desperately needed.
In your paralytic state
You could no longer
Guard the door from
The demons of your past.
Out they would pour.
The harrowing experiences
Where forgotten the next day,
But not for me.
I watched the statue of
Who you pretended to be
 Crumble before me.
I learnt there was nothing
I could do.
Whilst you pretended that
Nothing was happening.

Sometimes our ideals about things
Are more exciting than
What they actually are.
Sometimes the only disappointment
Is the fall from our expectations.
Into something more simple.
Sometimes we destine ourselves
For failure.

Your
"I love you"
Merely meant
"I need you around".
You couldn't survive
Without someone
Desiring you,
Showing your worthy
Of a constant bed mate
Whilst gaining emotionally stability.
Your
"I love you"
Meant
"I need someone to love me".

The women will forever do all the hard dirty parts of raising their children
Whilst the fathers are able to offer the fun.
They don't get remembered for the shouting or the loosing of their minds.
That's the mother's job.
Whilst the children bare their fathers face and their last name,
The mother will always be waiting in the side-lines to mother.
The children will not remember their mothers late night worrying.
The children will not remember the stress of their next meal, their clothes
Or the lacking of the home they lived it.
But they will never be able to forget the things that they felt
And the relentless unconditional love of their mother
When the day was done.

Sometimes it takes
Someone to say something
To trigger a memory
Back into your life,
Like a tornado ripping through
Everything you had built.
When you hear it,
It's like the memory was there
Waiting of the edge of my lips
To be spoken out loud.
I wasn't courageous enough
So instead I write.
I'll never forget the day
He took advantage of the
Small child I was.
The day that would
Forever shape my opinions
Of boys and men
Hiding in my subconscious.
The day I lost control.
Through fear I learnt
That if I didn't care about
My body they could have it..
..Because it didn't matter to me.
I never knew until now
That I did care.
I just didn't know how to gain
Back control of what should have always been mine.

When your privilege results in the sprouting of opinions
On matters you have no experience of.
Remember that your privilege is a blessings that is
hindering your growth.
You don't need to be the same person you was in
moments before clarity.
That my friend is your choice,
Like watching trees develop and grow inside a cage.
You are the tree and you are the cage.

I wanted to help,
I began to cut out parts of myself
And fill in your missing pieces with them.
I did this until I had just my shell left.
In that moment I realised I couldn't be the glue to hold
you together.
You didn't want to be fixed enough,
Your pain and experience were too irreversible.
I wanted nothing more than to give you more
But I had nothing left.
You left me the person I had met in you
All those years ago.

They are the multitalented,
They can maintain multiple personalities
And multiple faces.
Experts in the art of deception.
Hungry for the control and
The master of manipulation.
Their satisfactions are short lived.
They can't even live with themselves
Long enough before they change face.
Their skilled ability to avoid themselves
To not feel their own pain.
Whilst inflicting it upon others
Through their art display of multiple faces.

For as long as hate can reproduce
And the hunger for money is
More than the hunger for humanity.
World peace will be little more than a hope,
A distant wish in the hearts of the good.
Much like a child wishing for the genie to
Grant their three wishes.
As deserved as them wishes may be.
I learnt that we weren't served what we deserved
We were served the meal of the generation before.

Just like the flowers needed water, nutrients in their soil
and sunlight
Humans needed care, stimulation and love or they begin
to wilt.
They wanted to thrive amongst the 6ft sunflowers but
they were a reminder of everything they are not.
For they were given different chances at life.

I don't remember the exact moment when my heart
steeled over
Towards the opposite sex but I can remember all the
reasons why.
In a dream like state I remember the times I cared, I
loved so carelessly,
So passionately and so blindly.
I didn't think I needed to protect my heart from feelings
so pure.
Now I look back on my exposed self
And shudder at the thought of leaving myself wide open
To an arrow straight through the heart.
Not now. Now I am a warrior armed with my greatest
protection.
My heart of emotionless steel.

There are no others words to describe me at school
Other than a failure.
I couldn't fit in them parallel lines
And my heart didn't beat in the rhythm they needed it
too.
I tried my best to fit in to that tidy box
But my person was too colourful for that.
It wasn't until I was able to break free from expectations
 Of what I should be that I was really able to look
Into the mirror and see my honest reflection.

The remorseless words slipped from your lips
As effortlessly as the floated freely towards me.
Then they hit like a typewriter
Stamping the words straight into my heart,
Bruised from the words that I was told in song
Would never hurt me.
Whilst I feared the sticks and stones
It was the words that left me disfigured and
unrecognisable.
The words that left me harmed and my heart aching.
The words!
They forget to tell me that broken bones heal
But broken people don't.

Someone once told me I was beautiful
But she sensed I didn't like what my beauty brought with
it.
The presumptive behaviour,
The inability to see anything beneath my skin,
The expectations of whom I am.
She was right, I didn't.
I wanted women to be noticed for far more
Than the features on their face
And the assets on their body.
They are so much more than that,
Their intelligence,
Their unbreakable motherly instincts,
Their scarred hearts still full of love.
Beauty is luck, everything else is magic.

The pigment in my skin means that my hello is not as
sincere as your hello.
My melanin means that my intentions are interpreted
differently to yours:
No matter how pure I try to be.
My experience of injustice are brought upon myself
And my voice must only echo what they understand.
I have the potential to achieve but as far as they let me.
I can also be beautiful if I westernise my look,
I will remain at my level and not lay myself bare.
My straightened hair and contoured features are yours
and I must never forget it.
However your injected fuller lips and tanned skin are
also yours, because god forbid
That anything beautiful come from the lesser:
Than the talented, beautiful, powerful and wealthy team
That you are so privileged to belong too.
No, not me but I will have to be silenced before I deny
myself of the truth any longer.

Drip, drip, drip,
The therapeutic sound of the water dripping from the tap
 Into the water I lay submerged in.
As I battled between the peaceful place I lay and the
suffocating thoughts in my mind.
The salty tears screamed down my face
And began to pollute the purity of the water.
I began to feel guilty that once again
My feelings had spilt over into something else's
existence
And snatched what it was and changed them.

Some people just can't be alone,
No matter how hard they try
They find their identity in another.
Their security in someone's arms
And the worth dependable on
If someone else said their worthy.
These people are easy to spot
They are the ones who are with
Someone new before you realise
They aren't with their last and
No matter the excuses they give,
We all know the truth.
They know the truth.
They are the ones that seem so much
Happier than the rest of us
With their picture perfect illusions.
Whilst they go through the cycles
And fall in love with love and the
Temporary ecstasy it gives them
Again and again.
Whilst we take longer but we
Fall in love with ourselves and
Never get left empty.

Memories are like finding heavenly paradise
In a remote spot in your mind
Or like a branding iron imprinting you for eternity.
Warming or awakening you to never forget in innocence
What you had learnt from experience.

If this is love I don't want it.
Keep it! Keep it far away from me
And let me heal all the holes you picked into me.
Let me go back and remember that little girl I used to be,
The one with high hopes and aspirations for success and love.
She wouldn't be happy with what I had let her become.
Let me go back and try again.

It hurts as much now as it always has.
Feeling pain is inevitable and I wasn't immune.
My pain gave birth to my anger
But my anger had a control over me that
Made me feel helpless,
That made me feel like they had won.
I fumbled around in the dark for the emotions I
understood
But instead I found forgiveness,
Forgiveness for all my persecutors.
No, not because I was weak or I understood their ways
But because it gave me a strength,
A control over the uncontrollable
And an inner peace that couldn't be changed
Or be decided in the hands of the devil.

I never valued it back then.
Back when it was so readily available,
Back when they was your only ally and I expected things
to never change.
I woke up to the shattering of this phantom
Along with the harsh lesson I needed to learn.
People are not property and
They are not to be taken for granted.
She had given me relentless friendship.
I'll never forgive myself for my lack of responsiveness to
that towards the end.
In that moment I learnt that someone's true friendship
Was one of the most valuable jewels
 I could proudly wear.
A friendship that had no financial gain,
No control gain,
No sexual gain,
No miss placed loyalty.
It was purely based on her wanting me around.
I had no one else to blame for that.
I had gotten in my own way.

She was your loyal
Obedient dog.
Just how you liked her,
Just how you taught
Her to behave.
Her loyalty had become shackles,
Bound to your words.
A loyal companion
To your ever action,
Without question.
Like clockwork her
Actions became predictable,
Her personality drowned
In her loyalty for you.
So in tune with your needs
Her voice projected your thoughts
Through introjection.
Nothing could fail her service
As your loyal obedient dog.
For she loved you more
Than you even loved yourself.
Enslaved to the vows,
Till death we do part.

I do not believe
In a wrong time.
Two people who
Meet at the wrong time
Are just two people
Wrong for each other.
As perfect as things
Seem in a moment,
They are merely the
Capturing of beautiful moments
Collected as memories.
People who cannot live
Without each other mutually
Will settle for nothing less
Than the words forever.

I'm sorry for saying
Those mean words
That I did not mean.
Now I have seen their damage
But truthfully I meant every
Word of them at the time.
I meant for them to strike.
It was hindsight that
Caught me and branded me
With the truth.
It taught me that along with
Cruel words
You sign a declaration,
A memory
Scorned in a persons
Mind of damaging pain.
Along with their memory of you.
You can never be remembered
How you would like to be
Remembered again.

Her eyes glazed over to your empty promises
And even emptier heart.
She had let you in and promised herself your lies were
the truth.
She gave you every part of herself
And watched it seep through the cracks.
She couldn't convince you to love her probably,
You were just a boy.
A boy in gentleman's clothing.

Sometimes who I was,
Was uncontainable.
I was a person who's passion
Could erupt above the surface.
However sometimes the life
Would bleed from my cheeks
And I was grey.
I would blend within a crowd
Completely unnoticed.
Sometimes by choice,
Sometimes it chose me.
I wasn't the same person
Every day.
I was a product of every
Moment before the one
I am currently in.

I often wondered
Why I attracted the broken.
Now it all seems so crystal.
I couldn't be with a person
With less scars than me.
I needed to be understood.
The difficulty came between
Finding the healing and
Finding the irreversibly broken.

We live in a world so picturesquely beautiful,
No matter where you place your finger on the map.
It had given life and home to so many
And man cruel had not been kind.
With our ignorant excellence we used it to only benefit
ourselves.
Our greed to own everything whilst we concreted over
life.
The over valuing of things
And the undervaluing of each other.
We had so much potential in such a beautiful world.
Our beautiful heartbroken world.

My vision was weakened
By what I wanted to see.
My emotions were dissolved
By what I wanted to feel.
My hearing was impaired
By what I wanted to hear.
There was the truth.
Then there was me.

What happens if you take someone's vision away?
A good man remains a good man
And is felt with the heart.
What happens when you give them back their sight?
A good man becomes the colour of his skin
Because the only time equal means equal is in a maths
equation.

He told me that he loved me.
I had no reason not to believe him.
Maybe it was because I had always wanted
Someone to feel that way.
As time began to pass your behaviour
Revealed a sinister story.
Love didn't do those debilitating things
But you certainly did.
I decided that our expectations and conditions on love
were so drastically different or
Broken people can't love.
Both of us.

He leaned in intimidatingly towards me
And began to touch what he felt was his.
His touch repulsed me but I knew not to anger him.
I knew what was good for me.
It was perplexing to think that he could be
That cruel and expect me not to react to it
Because now he felt he was being nice, he wasn't.
Again he was getting his own way like he always had.
I had to be careful with every word I said
And every step I took as I knew he was watching me
Waiting for an excuse.
I became easier when I was paralysed with fear
I didn't need to be so careful.
I began to understand what provoked him
And I made sure I stayed clear.
I didn't want much it return,
I was wanted to leave alive.

There was one thing that made me unrecognisable,
Even to myself.
It changed my opinions of other,
It made me bitter,
It made me change.
It weaved into my mind and
Grew through all my dark places and lived there like ivy
on my soul.
It was something I hated.
I watched on as the person I recognised to be my self
Acted in ways I didn't recognise.
My duality wasn't pretty.
It only put my insecurities in the spotlight
And like a disease taking over my body I watched my
eyes turn green.
All in the name of jealousy.

As I foraged hopelessly, I released it was so hard now
To find a gentleman with a general respect women.
In a generation that sleep with someone they know nothing about
Because it's more acceptable than feeling anything to deeply.
When we really need someone to make love to our soul,
To devour everything we are.
To make us feel like we are worth the title, lady.
The sort of men I knew did have love to offer:
For their brothers but more blatantly themselves.
They find it easy to forget their existence is from a woman
And in that they forget a woman's worth.
My heart shattered watching on to our shared story.
I realised they wasn't the only ones to forget: in allowing this to happen,
So did we.

I felt lonely.
I had people around me but I had never felt more alone.
Stuck between the people who didn't see me
And the people who I was too afraid to tell them I didn't
want to be invisible anymore.
I didn't know how to change from the strong
independent woman they knew me as
To the vulnerable one I knew I was.
I needed to be seen
But no matter how many times I tried
To bold myself up and colour myself in I was still
See-through.
I wanted to scream,
I wanted to cry.
I wanted to be allowed to be weak.
Instead my fear of rejection won.
I locked my door to break down and only opened it
When I was ready to face the world with the person they
knew me as.

I watched on as you began to fade away
And your light went out.
There were no amount of truth that could change your
mind
And my efforts became hopeless.
You didn't want to be helped.
You cut all your lifelines and began to float away.
You became his duplicate
And whilst his strength doubled
Yours disappeared.
I mourned you.
I could see you in front of me but you no longer existed.

I had scars on my body
From putting myself in dangerous situations.
From ignoring good advice
From good people.
Scars from thinking that I knew best.
Scars from loving someone like you.

She was the nervous type,
Like a doll on the shelf who observed it all.
The one who overthought everything.
The one who would shake her foot to rock herself to
sleep.
The one who would wrap her fingers around her hair
 To try and distract herself from her worrying.
She would wake up abruptly with the weight of the
world on her shoulders,
And the reminder of some of her most painful memories.
Almost like if she thought about them enough the shear
agonising pain
Might be enough to change them.
Enough to gain some authority over the things she
couldn't control.
She knew it served no great purpose
But it was a part of who she was.
It was a part of the stitching that held her together.

There is something tranquil and releasing
About being comfortable in silence.
Then other days the silence made my thoughts ring
louder
And turned up my feelings
 Like the volume of my favourite song.

Being attracted to and compatible with a broken person
Said a lot about me.
However painful to admit.
I remind myself that birds never confuse themselves with aeroplanes.
Their different.

He asked me when I changed,
He didn't like the person I am now.
The person who was no longer a
Caged animal agreeing with his every word
And believing his presence offered
Me a better existence.
Now I didn't care and I was angry
Angry with the conditions he had left me in
And the lack of basic care and love.
Immediately he wanted the old me back.
No, not because he cared but because
He feared being exposed.
Exposed for the truth and he didn't like
The truth much.
The truth was too real
In his world of lies and illusions.

I believe they are in there somewhere
Frozen over for a better day
When I no longer had to protect them.
It had become excruciating to hurt that badly.
Survival numbed my heart to stop the pain
But it always continued to beat.
Hopeful that they would one day return,
Hopeful for a better day.

I couldn't move,
Frozen to the spot I was stood in.
It shook me all the way to my core.
It still felt human but I couldn't register
What was stood in front of me.
I was aware some people were passionate about their
hate
But maybe my innocence thought there was something
Human still left inside.
This time it felt different.
I could see it in their eyes.
As they glazed over into a death like stare so did their
humanity.
It was heart-shattering to think they could hand
something that personal over so easily, so carelessly.
Then that was it, there was no turning back.
Hate was too powerful once it had hold.
I watched on as their hearts turned cold,
As they became the dead, cold soldiers of hatred.

My head was hurting,
But it didn't break,
My soul was aching
But you couldn't see.
My eyes were tired
But they didn't cry,
And my emotions
Were beaten within
An inch of their lives,
But the damage was internal.
Now tell me again
Why is it that it's only true
If you can see it?
If only I had an X-ray
To prove to everyone
That my soul is broken.

I made friends with the dark
That I was once afraid of.
As a child I was petrified of what might
Be waiting inside.
I would hide from all the scary images of my mind.
I discovered as time passed that
The thing I needed to scared of were in plain sight,
They weren't afraid to be hiding in the dark of the night.
Now I hold hands with the pitch black
Whilst it offers me the safety of
Not being able to see the truth.

She ran silently whilst internally screaming
Hopeful not to wake the beast.
Like a magnet attracted to her calm exterior
And internal chaos it continued to pace forward
In her direction, she could sense it.
No matter where she would hide it would always find
her.
It had found her and others like her many times before
But she always imagined a time when she didn't have to
fear it coming.
She knew it could smell her fear and it made it angrier
than the time before.
Then it took hold of her like a thief in the night
And swallowed her whole.
The depression.
She couldn't escape it, it was a part of her.
So she waited till it spat out what was left of her.
Her strength began to repair the parts of her that it had
destroyed
Whilst she waited.
Waited anxiously for the next time it would find her.

She couldn't carry the burden
Of you any longer.
She carried you through
Whilst you cut her at the knees.
Her strength triumphed
So strong it was enlightening.
She was never really fixing
The broken person you are.
She was filling you,
Whilst you drilled holes into yourself.
You knew you was beyond help
So you was willing to weaken her
And drag her to hell with you.
Shame on you,
But now you know.
You can't drag good people
To dark places.
They do things that you could
Never understand.
They seek the light.

My wounds where deep
Like peering down
Through a monumental crack
Into the earth's surface
After a natural disaster.
Watching the earths
Internal core glow through
The destruction of its
Very existence.
It took my wounds to
Be able to get a glimpse
Into what I was really made of.
Anything of importance
Was deliberately hidden away
For only the hungry
And strong willed
To uncover.

The Therapy

Is writing healing me and helping my grow
Or leaving me vulnerable
As I open up a window into my naked soul.
The process of therapy can hurt
With the rawness of being honest
About who you truly are.
This feeling is the same.
The therapy of my pen.

When I speak with such passion
About the healing of poetry,
I was greeted with confusion.
They didn't understand how something like that
Could make me feel that way.
There was no other way to explain to them
Other than we all need a release from the hardships of
life.
Just as when their day was done they find
Escape at the bottom of a self-healing glass.
In much the same way I found my escape at the end of
my pen.

Touch me,
In places I've never been
Touched before.
The dark places
That people fear to go.
The broken cracks
That hold my deepest
Secret thoughts.
No one else
Can say they have
Touched me there before.
Be the first to have all of me.

Sometimes I go back in my mind and
Rewrite all my damaging memories.
I recreate them into something less painful.
The pain of the memory was always my greatest teacher
And recreation is what my teacher taught me I deserve.

I don't feel the same anymore,
I've changed.
I don't seek validation from another anymore,
Hell, I don't even feel anything.
I will not return to hell
I've been burnt enough.
I don't need to be loved
When I have learnt to love myself.
I am a self-fulfilling Queen
And Queens don't wait for life to knock on their door.
They go out and make it happen.

My mind holds the skeleton key
To all the wonders of my potential.
My Endless possibilities and
My greatest achievements.
I can lock it and stay safe where I am
Or open it and fly.

I want to be like the water.
No one can deny the beauty and peace it can bring
To wherever it graces itself.
Remembered for its transparency, its purity and tranquillity
But equally unforgettable for its tsunami like strength and
Its sole purpose in the evolution of life.
Mother Nature was always the greatest at picking the best leaders,
It is equal in strength as it is in beauty.
I want to be remembered that way.
I want to be like the water.

I paused for a moment and let time standstill,
I stood there looking up with my eyes closed:
Shutting out anything that wasn't happening in that exact
moment.
I smelt the rain before I felt it drip down and press
against my skin.
This time the rain didn't hinder my day,
It cleansed me and brought me back to the moment I was
in.
In a moment where I had nothing but the life in my veins
And the thoughts in my mind.
I had never felt more present, more alive.
The wet rain awoke my wilted soul.

I looked back on my former self
With displeased eyes and a squeamish stomach.
Who I was did not reflect my true likeness,
It reflected my rebellion after years of suppression.
I was following a forked off road into nowhere
Now I feel clean again, like the shedding of my skin.
Change is something that was unavoidable
When you look back and pity your memories
Rather than reminisce about them.
People said a leopard cannot change their spots,
They were right but I was a lioness who blended
In to paint an illusion that I was the same.

Once upon a reality, I met a man who treated me like a Queen.
He lay the world at my feet and stimulated my mind
Leaving me no gaps for doubt.
He waited for me when I needed time but
Time was not really what I needed.
I needed to hide.
I distanced myself further and further away till
He was no longer in reach.
I look back on that time with watery clouded eyes.
The only thing that was missing was the parts of me
That I didn't want to burden him with
He was looking for a Queen
And he mistakenly found a young girl playing dress up.
I couldn't pretend forever.

I noticed that people
Often connected
Anger with strength.
A person must have had
A difficult life
To be that angry and hurt.
Although there was truth
In that statement
I had noticed that
Forgiveness and inner peace
Were some of the most
Mind altering qualities
I had ever witnessed.
Whilst it was easy to be angry,
And being angry was their right.
It took a remarkable unnoticed
Strength to not choose it.
Or let it choose you.

It would not matter
How Glorious,
How spectacular,
How large
You feel the tree is.
The most astounding part
Of the trees journey
Was unseen.
How far and deep its roots spread
And how many strong
Connections the roots had made
Kept it standing far longer than
How beautiful you thought it was.

There were no words to define her,
She was an unusual type,
A limitless person of personalities and character.
She possessed both a heavenly heart and hellish attitude,
And oozed the power of both thunderstorms and
sunshine.
She was unpredictable to say the least,
But cliché she was not.
She was the colour in a black and white world.

He ceased all opportunities
That crossed his path,
With a carless grace
And a can-do attitude.
There was nothing that blocked his way
As his mind did not understand the meaning of limits.
I admired that, even more so because my mind
Didn't offer the same.
Mine created things to worry about and
It questioned my abilities.
Whilst our crossings were fleeting,
It taught me the importance of the power of self.

The most generous of people
Would give you their skin
To keep you warm.
Knowing it will leave them
With nothing but
Knowing it is no different
To what they had before.
They understand you
Cannot hoard feelings,
The only way to double
Their worth was to share them.
Turning them from coal to diamonds.

Watch them soar,
As my words take flight.
Envision the images they create.
I never fear that they won't return,
For my mouth is their home
And my pen is their podium
They will be seen.
They will be heard.
They will never be hidden again.

It took great strength to remain gentle
In a battle against the masses.
And for that she was a warrior.
A warrior seen as a weak link
To the blackened hearts of hate.

There are no games,
Just you placing barriers in your own way.
Just you separating yourself further away from the
inevitable.
The Truth.

Sometimes you will never get all the answers you desire.
You can continue to battle that or
Accept that not everything is in your control.
Sometimes it's with another and they decide how it goes.
The power wasn't always in the answers,
Sometimes the power was in letting go.

I want to fulfil
Every part of me, myself.
I do not want to rely
On anyone to make me
Feel complete.
That does not mean I don't
Want you around.
That means I don't need
You to complete me to make
Me whole.
Instead can our already complete
Souls dance together
Side by side.
Not because we need to
But because we want too.

As your former shallow puddle of depth evaporates
And out of your cocoon of motherhood comes
The grand canyon of worry and unconditional love.
The feeling that nothing will ever be more important
Than them people you created and in that moment
You are more connected to godly magic than any
moment before.

I bare the stretchmarks as a reminder that they were a part of my body.

They grew into people inside of me, we were two inside of one.

Really that close, both metaphorically and realistically and nothing could change that.

No matter how much they grew, they would always return home.

Not to the place but to the beating heart that nurtured them

And the warmth of the soul that comforted them.

To the arms that would protect them

And the stern that would guide them.

Most importantly to return the love to a person who they could never forget.

The person who was in their every memory

As their number one fan through the greatest of times and the hardest of battles.

I lost my appetite for love,
Whilst everyone else returned like starving zombies.
I enjoyed everything that they had left behind.

As I gazed out of my window
Into a world of infinite,
I asked myself why my feet
Were cemented to this one place
When I knew my heart beats for discovery.
My heart tightened and my butterflies
Revealed my truth.
The unknown may be frightening
But something I feared far greater was
The thought that my time will be up
Before I walk away from comfort
And discover what my heart beats for.

Writing has awoke me
In every sense of the word,
My senses, my silences, my beliefs.
I can't dial down my thoughts
Now they flood through me and out of me
Like a volcano of internal poetry.

He made my face hurt.
No, not from abuse or relentless crying but
From my uncontrollable smiling when he was around.
This was new to me,
It felt almost like he enjoyed me being happy.
I felt like he could see me,
I mean really, really see me
But this time instead of familiar past times
He didn't want to hurt me.
He didn't even want to feed me lies.
Instead he set me free and embraced me.
He was so refreshingly happy within himself that
He told me that he needed me to be more like me.

A strong woman
Is both powerful and submissive,
Possessing the ability
To understand when to use both.
She equally understands that
Not every battle is hers to be had.
Although born awake,
They awaken with every moment
Of their experience, turning the key
To unlocking their potential.
Their greatest fear lies within
Themselves and the capping of
Their strength.
The fear of leaving themselves
Open to the dangerous.
You cannot live inside their mind
Unless they let you in.
Their biggest gamble is not
In the hands of another
But their ability to read others correctly.
They understand the responsibility
Is within themselves.
Regardless a powerful woman
Will not stay down long,
Before she resurrects,
Even stronger than the time before.

To them I was no more than the decision I made.
A young single mother of no worth to our society.
Expectations were stapled to me like a notice board
Without any idea who I was.
They didn't see the mother I was
Or the children I raised.
Doing double the work
For half the credit.
I didn't fit in their picture perfect frame
Because after all there were only one way
To do things.
I gave my children all my time,
I love them unconditionally
I worked double the shifts to provide
And I gained less credit and double the abuse.
Whilst my children gave me double the love.
After all they knew how the real story went.
The story of their lives.

She was bottomless pit
Giving all of herself to others in need.
Aware that she was nearly empty
But hopeful that someone
Would care enough to refill her.
Refill her like she refilled them for all those years.

There were words
I longed to hear,
I needed the words to flow
From someone's mouth.
Describing every inch
Of who I was.
Someone to understand me
With no agenda of their own.
Now I wonder why
I searched for that person
In every place
My presence touched.
It was me,
I was who I was searching for.

She had an attitude
As sharp as a dagger,
Or as he liked to persuade her-
An attitude problem.
He didn't like that sting.
He failed to remember
All the reasons it was there.
Defending her and
Packing a punch.
She expected him to take it hard
Like a straight shot of whiskey
To wake him up.
Her attitude was razor sharp, sassy,
Powerful and strong.
It was everything but a problem.
It was everything that she is.

They told her she was too passionate
About a whole lot of nothing.
A whole lot of something
They couldn't understand.
Her fire didn't burn that bright
For no reason.
Their ignorance
Only ignited that fire more.
She wanted her vision for change
To burn so bright
They could only see that message
Every time they closed their eyes.
She knew it wouldn't come easy
But she knew she had
An undeniable passion
And a strong willed fire.

I cannot express how
Beautiful it is to see,
When people are stood upon and
Trodden in the ground,
Expected to stay down.
They rise up in all their glory.
As equally stunning
As they always were
But this time flourishing
In experience and scars,
And still they rise.

I noticed that some pain
Was intriguing,
They wanted to know your story.
But debilitating pain was scary,
If they didn't think you could carry
Your pain on your own
They would run as fast as they could.
Only the golden few will stop
And ask to help share the load.

What did I do to deserve this?
How dare you come marching in with
No apologies and begin to show me you care.
Stop breaking down my protected heart
With your persistence, you're weakening my amour.
I don't want to fall again, I have learnt from my
mistakes,
Stop leaving me no choice.
I worked hard to make sure I wouldn't hurt again
And just like that all my hard work was ruined
Snatched in your smile.

He was untouchable to the lessons
The world tried to pollute him with.
He knew his purpose was far greater
Than being a slave to his surroundings.
He gave up being a king to remain a gentleman.

She was as soft
As the petals of a breath-taking rose.
Whilst you had to watch out
For her thorns.
They was the reminder of
Who she could be.
Given the wrong circumstance.

I knew from the moment they
Were born that there wouldn't be another day
That I wouldn't spend fighting.
Fighting for the way I needed the world to be.
Fighting to give them the strength
To endure the world the way it is,
And battling to keep them
The way they are
Before the world gets a hold.

He called me a silly little girl,
It was a way to make me feel small.
I'd heard men like him say it before
With a superiority in their voice.
Didn't they know who women are?
We are the ones who
Birth and raise children.
We are the ones suppressed
But still shine victorious.
We are the invisible soldiers
Pulling through the daily struggles
Of what being born a woman brings.
We are women,
And silly we are not.
We are nothing short of incredible.

They say that I'm deep,
I dare to go there.
Jump into the uncomfortable
And explore its realms.
Whilst they dip their toes
And find comfort in being surrounded.
I get to swim the ocean.
Where there is darkness
But also a whole new way of life
That we never knew.

She wanted to inject some happiness
Under the skin of her sadness,
And shed her skin like a snake.
Revealing a new her,
One she could be happy with,
One she could be proud of.
She had been surrounded by people
Who had convinced her otherwise.
She couldn't see she was already
Good enough.

I never looked at love
As an emotion,
That was too temporary.
It was not something that would pass
And return attached to your mood.
Love didn't depend on your day.
It was strong, consistent
And one of its own.
It would remain and didn't rely on conditions.
It was something like we hear about
In fairy tales, magically enchanting.
Instead it was real,
And lived inside us all.

She was afraid of giving herself
To someone again.
She was afraid to want something
So much it took away her logic.
She feared placing her trust in someone,
Giving them the power to destroy her
And hoping that they won't.
Knowing her hearts desires
Had previously let her down.
It could be everything she had ever wanted,
But it could also be everything
She already knew.

She was surrounded by people,
People all of the same.
Bonding over the crossed wires
Of their identity.
She desperately sought after that.
She had tried to pretend
But she knew her identity
Was different and so did they.
She longed to belong
And would take anything offered.
It was better than feeling outcast.
She knew her time wasn't now
But she knew she would find it.
She would fit in like a missing
Puzzle piece to wherever
Her heart belonged.

People often told me
To be careful what you
Surround yourself with.
It will become you.
I often got this confused
With ignoring my pain
Because I didn't want to
Give too much attention
To the parts of my life that
I did not want to become.
I awoke to find that
I had ignored the parts
Of me that needed the most attention.
They would have healed quicker
Had they not been silenced.

There was something about you
That made me feel like a child.
Since walking into adulthood
I missed that over excited feeling.
You stole my thoughts, my words,
Leaving me stood there mute.
I wanted to introduce me to you
But I was hiding somewhere,
Away from the rejection you
Hadn't had chance to give me yet.
I'd over think every encounter
We had and think of a million ways
To enhance it.
In reality I could barely look you
In the eye in case you pierced a
Hole into my soul, or worse.
You could enlighten my
Happily ever after with reality,
And I was enjoying living in my mind
Too much to risk that.

Change can bring
On your growing pains.
Don't let that be the reason
That you stop.
All the late night over thinking,
All those tears,
All those times your heart ached
Shouldn't be for nothing.
Change can be painful
But staying in an equally
Painful place is not healing you.
Change doesn't offer comfortable,
Change offers transformation.

Just like that and through no energy
Of my own I watched on as I saw
Your life fall apart.
It wasn't something I had even wished
Upon you. Even if it was
Everything that you deserved.
You always painted your life in that
Superior lighting which only highlighted
Your fall from your throne more boldly.
It had always been in my nature to help
But not this time.
I had tried that endless times before.
This time someone else was taking care of things.
Someone who I'd heard about
Countless times before but to see her
In action was even more astonishing
Than I ever could have ever imagined.
Just like that you got what you deserved
In the hands of karma.

I built a wall to shield myself
From anymore damage.
Each memory left me bricks.
Bricks that I used to build the wall higher.
I often wondered if anyone
Would bravely climb it and free me.
I gave up waiting.
My skin was tougher now and I was
Armed with myself for backup.
Instead
I saved myself.
As I took down my fortress
Brick by brick.
I needed to see the world again,
I needed to feel the world again.

You need to forgive yourself,
You don't need to make yourself suffer anymore.
Your pain does not define you,
It was a requirement to your self-discovery.
Nothing more than experiences to
Show you how valuable you are.
It's difficult to see how wonderful things can be
If you're in the dark.
It's hard to remember they are there at all.
Just like you, whilst you focus on the broken fragments
You forget you are the mosaic,
A collection of small broken pieces which only add to
your masterpiece.

As we tear our muscles
To make us stronger
The pain is forgotten
In the vision of better.
Maybe our hearts are
The same.
Maybe we focused
Too long on the pain,
We forgot we were
Weaker the last time around.

Everything else can wait,
Till the birds have stopped singing,
The children have stop smiling
And my pen has stopped writing.
Life is too fleeting to miss the
Important things in life.

Now I have learnt
To love myself,
I couldn't fall in love
With someone who offers
Me any less than what
I already have.

It took me a while
But I'm here.
I'm at the door
Of self-contentment
Full of admiration and love
For the person
Who I've seen scorned,
Damaged and scarred
Along the journey.
The only one to see every
Moment and the effect
They had.
It took me a while,
But I am no longer searching
For parts of myself.
Now
I am finally home.

Thank You.

74602349R00072

Made in the USA
Lexington, KY
15 December 2017